Table of Contents

Whom this book is for.

This book is for 10-year-old me. Oh, this book would have been so cool for me. It has so many fun interesting things that I pondered about or wanted to know back then. This book also covers my blind-spots that prevented me from improvement.

o

This book is for the motivated game developer who is going to put a lot of time into game development regardless of the obstacles they come across.

o

This book is for somebody who wants something fun to read every night that immerses them in their craft. In our content-treadmill social media culture, it can be so fun and refreshing to read something that was not curated by or designed for an algorithm.

I will answer your questions!

Email me at `michael.gpq@gmail.com` and I will personally answer your questions to help you with game dev!

Because this is a big deal for my free-time, here's some rules and etiquette you should follow.

- Provide proof that you own this book. Either a picture of an awesome you with this awesome physical book, or a receipt (You'll need a receipt if it's a digital PDF). (If you checked this out at the library or borrowed from a friend, that's cool, you should still take advantage of this.)

- Whenever I ask a question to someone who is really good or I look up to, I make sure to spend a lot of time on the question before I ask anything. This removes the easy answers and proves that I'm willing to work hard and not just looking for trivial stuff. It also shows respect.

- I idealize spending 10 hours of effort for receiving a minute of advice from someone I look up to. That may sound extreme, but when what I receive is valuable, it's hardly enough. You decide how valuable what you receive is. If you find it valuable, you should intend to use it.

Nobody knows anything.

The oracle answered there was no man wiser than Socrates.

When I heard the answer, I said to myself, What can the god mean? For I know I have no wisdom. After long consideration, I reflected that if I could find only a man wiser than myself, I may go back to god with a refutation in hand.

So I went to see a politician with a reputation for his wisdom. When I began to talk with him, I realized he was not really wise, although many people thought he was, especially he himself. I tried to explain to him that although he thought himself wise, he really was not. The consequence was that he came to hate me. Several who were present shared this hatred.

So I left him, thinking to myself as I went that although neither of us really knew anything beautiful and good, I was better off. For he knows nothing, and thinks that he knows. I neither know nor think that I know. In this, I seem to have a slight advantage.

— *Socrates*, by *Plato*'s account of his final speech to the court of Athens, before his death (Based on translation by *Benjamin Jowett*)

There's lots of advice everywhere. Unsuccessful people are as adamant about giving advice as people who are successful. And even successful people can give bad advice, though they're a safer bet as there's at least some piece of proof.

Anything can sound like a good idea surrounded with positivity or excitement. Whether or not it is actually good for you can be a different matter from whether or not it sounds good.

My personal assertion, that I would disown if ever I found something better, is this. Reality is very complicated. We make conceptual simplifications to understand it, and these are lossy (like JPEG compression). Then we make lossy simplifications of those lossy simplifications, and it objectively starts to look like a very compressed JPEG image, but that is our world-view, so we don't see what's wrong.

Pictured: A twisted world-view.

Note the image. Imagine rolling a ball down these hills and valleys. The ball rolling is my brain learning and gaining knowledge. A "local minimum" is the bottom of a hole; imagine it represents having the perfect beliefs to do a particular thing well.

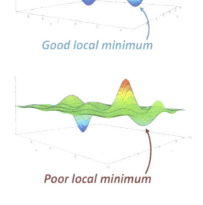

Good local minimum

Poor local minimum

Imagine the lower your "local minimum" is objectively, the better you can be.

Now imagine that if you wanted to be in a better local minimum, you would need to unlearn your current beliefs (going up the hill) to be at an objective vantage point that lets you pick a new direction to roll.

I think "good ideas" are just things that take us closer to our current local minimum.

Socrates has me think that this idea I share is not perfect but rather one possible way to view the world that may or may not help me.

This book contains a large variety of ideas. You may get excited about all of them. Throw away the ones that *end up* not helping you, and use the ones that do.

Practice makes permanent. Not perfect.

If I practice playing piano without pushing myself to understand what I'm doing, I won't become as good as I could be. I try to do the hardest thing, and I try to really understand it. I start from the middle of a random measure, remembering exactly which fingers should be where. I continue my internal metronome exactly from that point.

I don't simply start from the beginning and hope I play it better each time. Perfection can be a consequence, but it is not a given.

If ever there was a reason to do the best possible thing I can do to get better, it is the idea that whatever I practice now will become permanent.

On discovering a game development book.

As a young kid, I was very excited to get my hands on a copy of *Game Engine Architecture* by Jason Gregory. It's a reference book for making game engines! All games I know of have engines — exactly what I need!

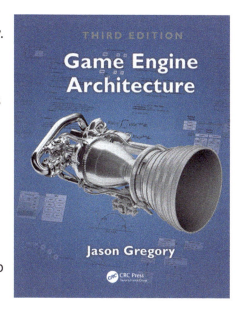

Well, I realize now it was a book for "engine programmers," not an "indie game developer" as I wanted to be. Much of the content are things I may never need to do in my life time.[1]

As a kid, I did not find it useful[2], despite much excitement.

---

1   My goal as of 2024 is to make games without engines, and my goal is not to make engines that others can use. Making that abstraction layer can be a life-long pursuit, and I am not currently interested.

2   I have since referenced this book for various things like implementing physics, but it was not what I should have looked at as a kid who wanted to make games. It is useful, but not for a kid who doesn't know what they need.

Designing Games was another book I discovered as a kid. I really enjoyed it, but I did not have the skills to quickly apply what I was learning (it truly is *design,* not development)

Tynan Sylvester

Designing Games

A Guide to Engineering Experiences

O'REILLY

As a reading, it was a valuable investment. 7 years later, I still remember various points from this book as I design my fun games with my own process.

o

This book you are reading right now, *Awesome Game Dev*, aims to give a mix of "valuable investment" advice that will help later, as well as stuff to get you going now, as that was what I really wanted as a kid but could not find.

This book will be helpful if you are excited about doing game development and put in your own work and research into your own projects. If you do not apply what you learn, then you're more of an enthusiast than one who gets things done.

Making a game that's fun.

This will be very specific to you and your creative voice. For me personally, I generally like to make the game fun first, and then add things around it that support that fun. Here's an example from my dev-logged *Fire and Flames* game for the TI-84+ CE calculator, written in C.

This game was very fun to play. Sometimes I would run the game to test something, and end up playing a whole level. Much of the development time was *after* the game was already fun.

I had a fun idea in my head that I knew I could make because of my experience with tangibly thinking of games in ways that can be programmed.

What if you could set fire to a building, then fire spreads to nearby tiles aggressively as you race your death to finishing the job?

The first few hours of working on the game gave me a tile-map with collisions. This was necessary for making the fun idea I had in my head.

On day 2 I made a lighter, napalm grenade, and flame-thrower. There were multiple floors (a 3D level in a 2D game), and fire would spread occasionally per "fire tick."

On day 3 the game was fun. Health and full levels. From then on, everything I did was in support of the fun. An external level editor for me to design in, a satisfying end-screen, a cut-scene intro, isometric previews in the levels elector. All of that is fluff that supports the fun thing my game does.

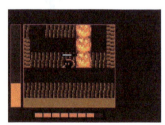

I'm sort of of the opinion that I should forget most things I learned and approach each project fresh. Otherwise my learned assumptions will become dead weight that will follow me to my grave.

Making a game that runs.

If you already have an idea of how you'll make your game, then you may not care for this chapter. But if you are confused on where to start, this will be a good read.

What is best for yourself is specific to you and how you want to do things.

Here's the deal. We're making games that run on computers. Being able to control a computer in such a way that runs your game can be pretty good. Learning exactly how the computer works so you can make games with it is invaluable. It is hammer-and-nail.

A lot of people like to make weird hammers that are meant to be child friendly (*Java/Javascript/Swift/Haxe*) or hurt the user when they try to swing it too fast (*Rust*). CPUs execute machine code. The C programming language translates to machine code pretty well, so it is a good tool.

If you use something that is not well-tailored to making interesting games, you run the risk of not being able to make something interesting enough to succeed in such a saturated industry as game development, nor may you feel fulfilled in your hard work. However, if a simpler tool like the Godot game engine can support everything you need, then it may be worth using. I compare and contrast two prominent developers' thoughts on this on Page 59.

o

I recommend Raylib with C so you can get simple input, window, and drawing code with little effort. When I was a beginner, this is what I wanted, and it is not bad. But if you were to use the internet to research how to use C (as I would find completely reasonable), you may find unreasonable results.

For example, they may tell you to use a complicated build system *that makes a build system* that builds your game (*CMake*). You may find people telling you to encapsulate everything into an Application class, and then make an Entity class which has an update function, then start using inheritance to make entity types. Now, all of a sudden, you are not allowed to have 1,000,000 entities update per frame because your game is too slow! Wouldn't that have been cool! For a beginner, a lot of the things people say will hurt their experience. It's not much harder to have done it well (though hardness should not dictate what we do).

I would like to save you some pain. First, C++ can be a waste of energy for a beginner.[3] Use C instead.

---

3   You can use C++ later when you think you're able to do things well without it. C++ has some handy things. But starting with it and its standard library can allow you to waste your energy on the wrong things just because it allows you to (To avoid: classes with functions inside them, C++ standard library, templates).

On Windows, compiling C code can be as simple as running an executable from the command-line (in this example, giving it a text file "main.c" to convert into a program): `cl.exe main.c`. It does not have to be as complicated as modern resources make it out to be.

One.

I set up a kit for people who want to develop with Raylib and C on windows. It should work on Windows 10 and Windows 11 without any pre-requisites.

Try the shorter URL tiny.cc/devkit or otherwise download from here: https://drive.google.com/file/d/1lvxkV-7zV3pbvgmnmCYAZCcymQUSYePB/view (120 MB)

Or two.

I highly recommend you follow along with Day 1 of Handmade Hero[4] to get a feel for setting up build environments. It will be a good use of an hour. There's also a useful "introduction to C" series there if you are new to the C programming language.

(If you want to achieve mastery, having a daily ritual to go through Handmade Hero for an hour would give you an incredible head-start. It's serious good stuff. It may

---

4   https://handmadehero.org/

seem like a long series, but I only wish it would last forever. The idea is long-term exposure (osmosis) to subtly transform your brain to become like that of the teacher. It'll save time. _This is the best possible thing you can do_. One-and-a-half hours per day.)

Or three.

You can also try the Odin programming language; I disagree with some of its principles, but it is quick to go from writing in a text file to having an executable file. In having a fresh compiler ecosystem, Odin is nicer than C.

As I write this, the _JAI_ programming language is not released. But if as you read this it is released, then I highly recommend it. It exhibits principles that I have personally found to be good for making games. Tiny standard library. Code is malleable. Low resistance. Low level; working directly with memory and the computer that it's running on. Building it is easy. Learning to make games with something such as _JAI_ is a good long-term investment.

Reading this book versus being successful.

> It sounds like you're already making lots of things, which is the important thing. Work a lot, make a lot of stuff, and try hard to make it really good. Everything else is tactical details, which will vary a lot according to your personal circumstances.

— *Tynan Sylvester* (*RimWorld* developer), to me via email.

It would be cool to gain the skills and ability to make cool games. Something I like to think about is me in 10 years. I think about them reflecting. What was it like? How did they get as good as they did? Never do they think, "I came upon a hard challenge, so I gave up."

Most people are satisfied with *good enough*. Most people are not super good at game development. I never existed in a society that supports mastery.

The closest I got to that "society" was luck on an online forum finding a particularly passionate programmer with low level C and assembly skills. I learned a lot from the little I heard from them, though I also learned that passionate skilled people can say a lot of things, and only some of it is necessary to get where you want to be (the rest is fluff).

I don't know of any good communities for being really good at game development. I know of communities where one can make friends and be excited about game development[5], but not everyone is really seeking to hone their craft and release things and do it well. In that case, it's fun to create new communities, whether they are small & private, or large & public.

O

---

5   As of 2024: *Handmade Network, Tigsource, Cemetech, Gamedev.net*

Communities can be helpful because you can feel a friendly rivalry that pushes you all to do better, or you can feel a sense of belonging that makes it easy to do work. Of course, if that community goes away, you need to overcome the loss of that and keep going. Exist independent of societal factors, otherwise you can only ever be as good as them.

I feel sorry for the developer of *Cube World*. Very nasty personal things were said to him by an entitled pitch-fork mob. I do not want to depend on a society as self-righteous as that.

o

Existing independent of input is another thing. Will you always depend on resources to tell you what to do? What if what you want to do is more complicated than anyone has ever tried before? Wouldn't that be cool and new! It would be a shame if you couldn't execute that idea.

Input is helpful. In a short life-time, it can teach us fundamental truths that we would have learned anyway (although beware of dogma such as "Object Oriented" being the *single best way* to make programs; that is *not* remotely grounded in reality). But it should not be *relied* on.

If I can only ever do what I have been told I can do, I would be bored.

O

You'll discover many resources that will supplement your journey. You'll also discover many that will hurt your journey. It is often hard to distinguish them. It will be awesome to find the good ones. This book will point to many things I found cool for my journey, but you'll also find many cool things that support your unique journey.

O

I try to only take advice from people who have proven themselves. If someone is saying something that sounds good, but it hasn't helped them achieve what I want to achieve, then it's not good. And sometimes people don't know why they succeed, so they'll put you on their inefficient path and you'll inherit all of their dead-weight assumptions as well. This can be an issue with taking advice from intermediate people. In order to achieve mastery, one must cast off dead-weight assumptions.

Many people who make a living from educating can give bad advice. They haven't succeeded themselves, and so how would they know what advice works and what doesn't? By testing it on students?

I avoid YouTube channels by people whose sole job is to make tutorials.

I covet the opportunity to watch an interview with someone who does the work that I want to do.

This isn't to say intermediate people and teachers are *bad*. They can be motivational or fun. They can be experienced enough to point to good resources that you may independently weigh for yourself. Just don't *blindly* trust everything that I or someone else says, unless they're doing *exactly* what you want to do at the level you want to do it.

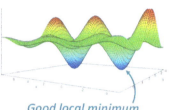

Good local minimum

The ideas intermediate people share may be exciting. They may even *help* that person do what they do. But they are an intermediate person, and for them to achieve mastery, they may have to un-learn that very idea in order to achieve a greater

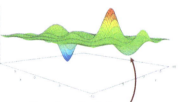

Poor local minimum

space of possibility. So, beware of advice shared by people who aren't absolutely excellent.

o

You might consider sending letters or emails to people you look up to. I've done this various times in my life. Email is magical. I should probably write physical letters; the fact that I haven't gone through that effort makes me feel like I must approach with even more respect. There's more magic to a physical tangible thing that was touched by the pen of the very writer. I would not dare waste the time of someone I look up to. If you send a message to someone you admire, do so from a point of respect, and don't try to only take; hope that they can enjoy their day having read your letter. If I send a message and they do not respond, it's not like I *deserved* a response anyway. If I receive a response, it's a *gift* and I feel appreciative. I recommend you treat them like regular fallible people who deserve respect like anyone else.

Never ask them a question they've already answered in an interview or in a blog somewhere, unless it's really really hard to find.

Drawing a player

When I was new to game development, I quickly found my local minimum of possibility: store the player as a rectangle at a position on the screen with a width and height in pixels, then draw that rectangle.

Somewhere, I globally made player X and Y variables to represent its screen position, then I made player width and height variables to know how big its hitbox is and how big to draw it. It looked vaguely like this:

```
float playerX = 0;
float playerY = 0;
float playerWidth = 20;
float playerHeight = 20;

int main() {

    while(true) {

        // ...there's lots of other game code...

        DrawRectangle(playerX, playerY, playerWidth, playerHeight);

        // ...

    }

}
```

Soon after, I wanted cameras that move with the player. The existing system would no longer do. If the camera moves 10 pixels right, then where do I draw the player? Well, if the camera moves right, the player will move left until they're off-screen. I found I could subtract the camera's position from the player's position to find where to draw it. It looked vaguely like this:

```
float playerX = 0;
float playerY = 0;
float playerWidth = 20;
float playerHeight = 20;
float cameraX = 0;
float cameraY = 0;

int main() {

    while(true) {

        // ...there's lots of other game code...

        DrawRectangle(playerX - cameraX + gameWidth/2, playerY -
cameraY + gameHeight/2, playerWidth, playerHeight);

        // Offsetting the camera position
        // by gameWidth/2 and gameHeight/2 makes (0,0) the center.
        // I did this in all of my old games.

        // ...

    }

}
```

Everything in the game world was drawn like this. With everything offset by the camera in the same way, it looked like a camera was really moving around.

Over the years, I found my local minimum of possibility was limiting. I struggled with making 3D games when I was young. I did not understand coordinate systems. I didn't know that there was an alternative to working in pixels on the screen.

It can be useful to think of different types of coordinates. World-space, and screen-space. You can make 1 unit in your game become 100 pixels on the screen. You can zoom your camera in and out by changing how you convert from world-space to screen-space coordinates!

For example, you may have a conversion function like this:

```
struct Vector2 {
  float x;
  float y;
};

float cameraZoom = 80;
Vector2 cameraPosition = {0,0};
// In the code I'll assume player's position is at his center
// and his "size" is his radius
Vector2 playerWorldPosition = {0,0};
Vector2 playerWorldSize = {1,1};

Vector2 screenSize = { 1920, 1080 };

Vector2 screenFromWorldSpace(Vector2 worldSpace) {
  Vector2 screenSpace;
  float offsetByCameraX = worldSpace.x - cameraPosition.x;
  float offsetByCameraY = worldSpace.y - cameraPosition.y;
  screenSpace.x = ((offsetByCameraX)*cameraZoom);
  screenSpace.y = ((offsetByCameraY)*cameraZoom);
  screenSpace.x += screenSize.x/2.0f;
  screenSpace.y += screenSize.y/2.0f;
  return screenSpace;
}

int main() {
  while(true) {

    // ...there's lots of other game code

    Vector2 playerWorldBottomLeft = {playerWorldPosition.x -
                                     playerWorldSize.x/2.0,
                                     playerWorldPosition.y -
                                     playerWorldSize.y/2.0};
    Vector2 playerWorldTopRight = {playerWorldPosition.x +
                                   playerWorldSize.x/2.0,
                                   playerWorldPosition.y +
                                   playerWorldSize.y/2.0};
    Vector2 playerScreenBottomLeft =
        screenFromWorldSpace(playerWorldBottomLeft);
    Vector2 playerScreenTopRight =
        screenFromWorldSpace(playerWorldTopRight);

    DrawRectangleWithCorners(playerScreenBottomLeft,
                             playerScreenTopRight);

    // ...

  }

}
```

This code allows you to arbitrarily zoom a camera. This was something I was completely unable to do for my first few years programming. By finally forcing myself to write game code in a 3D world, I was *forced* to make a system more complex than this, and so I now find this trivial to write. It may seem hard, but you just have to keep making things and it will come over the years, permanently for your use. Push yourself beyond what you know.

o

When I said I used to draw the player as a box, I also had that be his hitbox. I would use that for collisions. But one day I wanted to draw a picture instead of a box. This picture didn't necessarily have to fit the player box,

especially if I wanted an isometric look where only their feet would collide with the world. There *can* be a decoupling of rendering and hitbox, I found.

For example, in *Journey to Royn*'s tile system, tiles have visual and collision models.

Code that draws the tiles uses the visual model and adds the tile's position to the model to place it in the world.

Code that checks for collision uses collision model and adds the tile's position to each collision box.

Rest to learn

I asked a professional pianist for advice on learning. They responded with one particular point: you learn not when you're spending hours practising, but when you are resting. There are diminishing returns on practising for many hours at once, and the learning will only be visible after resting and starting again.

If you spend too many hours practising, you may lose energy and start doing things wrongly. Then, when you are resting, your brain will make connections based on how you practised. So, if you practised wrongly, then you will learn worse than someone who practised correctly. It's *possible* to practice less and learn more. But *as much as possible* is a good target. Too little will simply make it take too long.

In programming, we're changing our brains to think about how logic and code make a program run. There's systems in the brain that learn and grow much as a pianist grows rhythm and "muscle memory" and dexterity.

Just give me a draw rectangle function. I will make the game.

In modern computing, it is very difficult for a beginner game developer to make a window and start drawing things to it. In my game *Journey to Royn*, just creating the window and initializing the OpenGL context takes 366 lines of code. Right now, that is 1% of the project's code. But in the first day of the project, that would have been 100% of the project's code! A beginner that does not know there is light at the end of the tunnel may be overwhelmed while writing this initialization code — I was.

Resources I found turned me to making web games. At least then, I could throw in 20 lines of boilerplate and then already use `ctx.fillRect(playerX, playerY, playerWidth, playerHeight)` in a loop to draw a rectangle player per frame. From here, one could make all kinds of fun and interesting games.

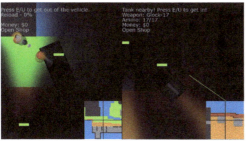

Stick Battle. A birthday present for my father that we enjoyed together. A web game. I had experimented with drawing transparent circle gradients into an opaque lighting canvas to make a daylight cycle.

Right now, if you do not know the way you want to make games, I would recommend you use the Raylib library with the C programming language. This will give you window initialization, user input, and plenty of functions to draw things for you.

You are an artist starting with a basic pencil. Pencils are just one way of doing art, and they can be expressive.

o

When you are more advanced, you could want your own "draw rectangle functions." You can do per-pixel shaders to make 2d art-work respond to lighting as if it's 3d (with hand-painted normal maps)! You can distort things. You can make rainbow squares. You can give *one* command to the GPU to draw 1,000,000 tiles (way faster than calling a generic "draw rectangle" function 1,000,000 times; your game will be smooth) This, along with fun gameplay, will allow you to make a good cohesive experience that is built entirely to support itself.

Fun gameplay with little emphasis on graphics has its niche (*Dwarf Fortress* is a particularly successful game, its lack of graphics playing into my imagination).

Bad gameplay with good graphics is known as "AAA" (big-budget studios avoid taking risks that would make interesting games, instead opting for what has been done before). Walking simulators also fill this niche.

Most people want fun gameplay with a nice graphical experience. Otherwise, I might look at a painting instead of playing a game. Painting is a good medium for visually pleasing static imagery. Hand-drawn animation is a good medium for moving imagery. What can games do better than painting or animation?

Stop trying to answer all the questions.

The previous chapter ends on the sentence "What can games do better than painting or animation?"

I know some people in my life that read that would read that question, think for approximately 4 seconds, then respond, "Hmm, well, games this and games that, but animation this and animation that."

Question such as this should require your whole *life*! Not 4 seconds. Yet they speak so confidently! Worse, if they ever think about it again, they think about it through the perspective they generated 4 seconds after hearing it.

The question is complicated. It's one that you can reset to a blank slate and then answer all over again with a different answer, as long as you do not dip into your preconceptions. The question is useful as an unanswered question that one can come back to. Those that think *The Trolly Problem* has a definitive answer miss the point. To me, it offers a way to think. It's an experience.

Don't need many tools.

If you have a C compiler, a text editor, and a terminal, then you can make really cool games. You don't need *Visual Studio*, and you don't need *Visual Studio Code*, and you don't need a *JetBrains* IDE.

A debugger can be helpful; I use RemedyBG[6] ($30). Perhaps when you are reading this, Rad Debugger[7] will be past its public alpha and useable. Visual Studio Community Edition is free, but it takes a long time to start up, and the UI is very laggy, so it's not very high quality.

o

Tooling for games can be fun! Some people make their levels based on images, where specific pixel colors become specific tiles. Other people make them based on text files, where specific characters map to specific tiles. My current project, *Journey to Royn*, uses a PNG for mapping biomes on the world map. This means I can use *Aseprite* or *Microsoft Paint* as my biome designer tool. Green means grassland. Yellow means desert. Red means corruption.

6   https://remedybg.itch.io/remedybg
7   https://github.com/EpicGamesExt/raddebugger

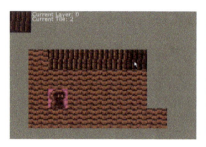 

In *Fire and Flames*, a game made in two weeks for the TI-84+ CE calculator in C, I made a level editor in HTML that exported directly to C.

```
level_t Level =
{{{0,0,0,0},{0,0,0,0}},0,2,3,0}
```

In *XTreme Golf,* I designed levels as C structs. Then, I made an in-game on-calculator editor that I kind of maybe intended to use for real level design.

Then I ran a level design competition and made a fancy playable HTML5 editor that implements the game's ruleset. Because other people were intended to use this, I made it feel nice to use. It exported level codes like this: `5AJA53AIKAQN3AIAIAVEAD5AI3AI6AGA`

—which is a simple run-length compression (GGGG becomes 4G) combined with turning combinations of tiles into single ascii characters (such as replacing every "3G1W" with "L").

The quality of tooling we have for designing our games has a big impact on how the game plays. I like making tools and then using them. It can be a big thing to re-invent photoshop or Autodesk Maya, and it may be a waste of time, but there are some things that can be tailored to making a game as good as it can be. Being forced to use generic tools for level design (like *LDtk*, *Tiled*, or *OGMO* for tilemaps) forces your game to be as uninteresting as those editors allow (which may or may not still be interesting). With those editors, it's a *bonus* to be able to make level triggers, not a *given*.

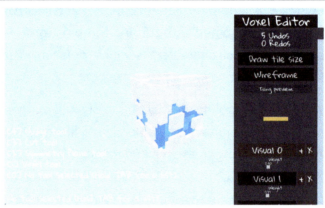

Royn's tile modeler works with exactly the format the game needs

Royn's level editor allows for terrain editing

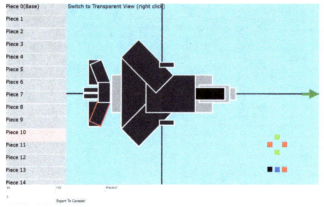

Stick Battle's vehicle modeler, exports to JSON array

There was another *Stick Battle* — a side-scroller version without vehicles — made for my father's birthday. It was very fun to work on and play. It also has its own level editor.

As a web game, it exported to JSON too.

You would press "W" to place wood, "G" to place grass, "R" to place rock, etc. The console tells you that it worked.

The top-down version of *Stick Battle*, also made for my father's birthday, worked similarly. Along with its vehicle modeler shown a few pages ago, it also had a level editor. One would press "G" for grass, etc. Zooming with the mouse wheel would change the minimap scale.

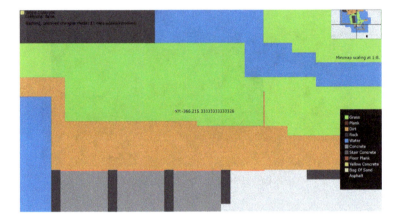

Making tooling that perfectly fits what a game needs to be its best, cohesive self can be useful. Making that necessary tooling poorly can be detrimental.

A digital painter uses *Photoshop, Procreate,* or *Clip Studio Paint*; they do not punch in the number values of each pixel's Red/Green/Blue channels one-by-one. It enables them to think on a higher level. This is why I make tools for games. So I may think on a higher level as a painter does.

Game loop.

Most games simulate themselves like this.

```
int main() {
    // Game started
    while(game_running) {
        // Code in this loop runs once every frame
        collect_user_input_from_operating_system();
        simulate_game_world();
        submit_draw_commands_to_graphics_card();
        swap_draw_buffer();
    }
    return 0;
}
```

You can do a lot with a game loop that looks like this. But you can also break free from this and do other cool stuff. There's a ton of freedom. This is just one way.

To express shock that one can make a game without object orientation.

No, just because *RuneScape* and *Minecraft* are object-oriented, does not mean your game must be.

Yes, many games have been made without object-orientation. I believe that if one embarks on a solo project, they are more likely to finish it if they do not adhere to object-oriented principles.

Yes, instead of making a scene class with an update function, you can just use a switch statement.

Yes, instead of making your entities polymorphic classes, you can just use a switch statement.

I don't understand this behaviour. Why should one think they need to use object-oriented ideals to make games? I've heard it as dogma in code reviews[8] given by intermediate programmers. They believe object-oriented is a strict measure of good code quality. It's just so detached from reality, I can't believe it. I fell for it as a beginner too, detrimentally, only because I believed what I heard without tangible grounded experimentation.

---

8   I can't mention code review without also mentioning that I find them a waste of time, and that if code cannot be perfect, it may be swapped out for something better when the time comes. And you can't polish poop and end up with anything but poop. It must be cohesively good, not nit-picked until it's good.

I still deeply cringe, remembering hearing a beginner programmer writing, "I don't know very much about programming, but listen, if you're going to be a good programmer, you're gonna *have* to write object-oriented code." There isn't a word to express the mental strain I feel. I can only hope that they learn to disagree with this statement they have made.

"Game programming patterns" as wasted energy.

When I was newer to programming and learned about game programming patterns, it felt as if the universe had turned on its head; I could finally break free of my amateurish habits and write code that makes real games! That didn't happen.

A programming pattern book may tell you that you can make an "observer pattern." You subscribe observer classes like it's a newsletter, and now the physics code can simply say "player hit ground at 200 units of speed" without worrying about who will receive it; you don't need to have achievement code that activates where physics code does! But now your code is more complicated and indirect, and did you solve any real problems?

Wasted energy. There's a chance this pattern helps a 500-person team where they want to strictly divide work (Bob Nystrom, author of *Game Programming Patterns*, claims to have written the book by observing development at *Electronic Arts*, a massive AAA studio), but this is only a hindrance to a small team of skilled programmers.

It's not a sin to have achievement code in your physics code, no matter what anyone may tell you. The achievement is based on a physics event. It is the most

1:1 representation of how the program *should* run. Perhaps this is a human error, that one thinks code should not reflect how a program runs best but rather how they think; so, they change the program and make things happen less directly because they're so fond of indirection.

Another example of this is Entity Component Systems (ECS). You could be direct, or you could force a square-peg through a round-hole for benefits that you don't even get as an indie developer. ECS is used by engine developers because that's the interface they give developers as people who don't know how their engine will be used (because they're making an engine, not a game). If you are writing a game that just needs to be a game, not a generic interface, then write a game, not a generic interface.

It's so exciting! ECS! But at the end of the day, I need a game that runs and does interesting things, and it could objectively be written faster and more cohesively if I don't try to shoe-horn a data-structure that doesn't solve any tangible problems that actually matter.

It's not actually exciting. It's just as exciting as any idea people bring up nowadays. ECS! Observer pattern! Borrow-checker!

How much work did you get done today? How much of that would you consider is "necessary groundwork to get the job done" versus actually getting the job done? I'd like you to re-consider what constitutes <u>necessary groundwork</u> because so many people assume they need to do things that they really don't. They box themselves in with assumptions. Actually getting the job done is what matters, and the path we take to get there can be any. It doesn't need to be the complicated one.

o

Besides, learning programming patterns with the intention of applying them like tools in a toolbox is inherently non-ideal.

If every problem is unique and has a best possible solution that uses primitives such as code and memory, then why limit ourselves to a subset of 10 applications of code and memory (programming patterns) and find the best fit? Why not make something bespoke using the basic tools we're given?

https://commons.wikimedia.org/wiki/ File:India_-_Varanasi_tailor_-_0619.jpg

This takes effort, so you may not want to do it. Doing this, we may sometimes converge on a known programming pattern anyway. Or we may discover something new and better that doesn't have a name yet. I think instead of learning existing programming patterns to use them, consider learning how to *make* programming patterns as needed to fulfill a task.

Don't be satisfied with an answer.

If someone shows me how to do something correctly, I wonder how I could not have come up with that on my own. I wonder how many other things that I am currently not coming up with because I have not seen someone show me. I wonder how limited I am in what I can do.

I wonder how I could have come up with it myself.

This is taking issue with being dependant on my input, because if I can only do what is shown to me, then how could I ever accomplish something interesting or new? In the last chapter, I showed how one could use coordinate systems to zoom a camera. However, I did not show how one could come up with this themselves without prior knowledge.

I don't know the best way to think to solve problems. I wouldn't recommend just doing it the way that works for you because maybe the way that it works for you is non-ideal, and it might be better to change yourself so that you problem-solve better. It could be either way.

So, all I can say is this is a thing that will be personal to you, and you will have to go through resistance to find out how to do things well.

Be true to your craft, without pretensions.

Be true to your craft, Without pretensions. Even though we're creating entertainment. Like it or not, a film is reflection of its director. There's no getting around that. Regret comes from having not made a film true to my heart. I would not be able to make another film ever again.

— Hayao Miyazaki (*10 Years with Hayao Miyazaki*)

This quote was powerful for me. Often my emotions get in the way of doing what I know is good.

It is like the willingness to scrap a project a year in because you realize it is not as good as it can be. No pretensions. No sunk-cost emotions.

It ignoring feeling embarrassed doing the correct thing.

If you feel like your game would be cool with something, but you do not want to do it because it would be hard, that is your pretension getting in the way of something great.

o

I was looking at old videos of mine for a different part of this book, however I stumbled a video of me playing *Minecraft* when I was 9 years old. In this video, I see I changed all of the localization texts to my own custom phrases. Such as in the command-block interface "Done" becoming "Finished? click here" and "Cancel" becoming "What! no dont cancel!"

As I was looking at this cancel option, I couldn't help but remember this chapter's title. "But clicking cancel is what I need to do because I messed up the command!" I think to myself. But the button begs not! Furthermore, I had made it beg not by changing the localization texts!

The best thing to do would be to hit cancel, and to perceive it as "Cancel."

Check-the-boxes mentality.

"I studied for the test! Why didn't I get a good grade?"

You can do all the things that someone successful has done and not succeed. After long investment you may feel indignant, or cheated. "I tried to write a screen-play, and I used the 3-act structure, why don't people like it?"

"I tried to compose music, and I used existing song structures with well-known chord progressions, why is it not famous?"

"I tried to make a game, so I added all the systems games have with an inventory and crafting and fighting, why isn't it popular!"

Inventories and crafting systems and 3-act structures and song structures are all completely coincidental to success and may only create a "contemporary" style of something good or bad. (Famous ancient stories did not necessarily use 3-act structures. And not all writers who converge on a 3-act structure were necessarily *thinking* of conforming to a structure.)

o

"I did the things the society told me to do, and I did not gain success, either in making something good, or making something popular, or both."

There are factors way beyond what society tells people to do, and what society tells people to do is often only the means to reaching mediocrity.

Perhaps the mentality should not be to check the boxes — it should be to make something good, and deliver a good experience to end users. Whether or not any "boxes" get checked is coincidental and irrelevant.

Checking the boxes is not thinking deeply about the consequences of actions.

I used to have the traits of this character. I would do as I'm told and hope it results in something good. I know people in real life who are like this. When I realized this, I changed myself very quickly to avoid it.

Structure is a square-peg, round-hole.

I remember hearing Jonathan Blow discussing auto-correct and proof-reading tools. This was my take-away; Grammar correction tools exist. But if a native speaker with a good grasp of the English language uses one, then that may just reduce the height of quality that this person may reach via writing.

In *Lord of the Rings*, J.R.R. Tolkien often lists characters by writing "Frodo and Strider and Gandalf and Merry and Pippin." A grammar checking tool will see this and adamantly replace it with "Frodo, Strider, Gandalf, Merry, and Pippin." I find this tragic because the former way of writing has so much more child-like wonder and energy than the latter. The latter is adult-like, academic, and bland. This extends beyond child-versus-adult style writing. I think this is the expressivity of the language that is suppressed. A native speaker knows how to bend the rules to increase clarity or play into voice.

Grammar correction tools may make it easier for a fool to not mess up, but it makes it more difficult for a genius to go as high as they will.

In other words, they raise the skill-floor, and they lower the skill-ceiling. One may fail harder, but they may succeed more.

And in a society of 8 billion people, I believe it more useful to increase the overall number of highly-successful cases instead of keeping everyone in the same bracket.

o

University has about 3 months to teach you something, and then the class is over and another class must take its place.

I remember hearing Marshall Vandruff mention that as a college teacher, he wished he could split classes into "three acts" instead of the prevalent first-semester "A" and second-semester "B" system.

I believe that fielding numerous students through one system is not the best way to give any one of them mastery.

For the individual, I don't believe a system designed for hundreds of people is nearly as good as one system designed for one person.

University is too loved.

> Nobody ever asked to look at my degree

— James Gurnie, Age 64, artist, author of *Dinotopia* (https://youtu.be/5xkn7VWdKZ8?t=1427)

> I have never been asked where I went to school

— Terryl Whitlatch, Age 62, scientific and academically trained illustrator, creature designer for *Star Wars* (https://youtu.be/UjVk4R02PyY?t=4051)

> I wouldn't recommend going to school necessarily. It's so expensive, and there are so many better ways to learn things, that I'm not sure it's a good choice.

— Jonathan Blow, creator of *Braid* and *The Witness* (https://vimeo.com/934338840)

> I didn't write a single piece of good code for five years. Once I finally unlearned everything from college, I started programming correctly.

— Casey Muratori, creator of *Granny* animation tool used in thousands of games, programming educator (https://guide.handmadehero.org/code/day023/#6126)

> *No great artist ever graduated from college.*

— N. C. Wyeth (1882-1945), renowned illustrator.

"[To me,] a college degree means practically nothing"

— Casey Muratori
(https://guide.handmadehero.org/code/day211/#4129)

I literally have many emails of people saying "Watching the first few episodes of Handmade Hero, I learned more than I learned in four years of university." Why? Because actually that's just a better way of educating. You take someone who knows the thing you want to do, you watch them do it, and you no longer have to go to a particular physical location to make that be true. So, in my mind, universities are probably single biggest societal problem facing us today. They are an entrenched, costly, ineffective system that is at the root of all major industries... In my mind, the solution is to completely replace them.

— Casey Muratori, (https://youtu.be/Sj3MnsHznGI?t=6834)

Jack of all trades.

Games are very complicated. I cannot reduce it to core parts correctly, but perhaps I can demonstrate its complexity.

Largely there's game design, visual design, and sound design.

Visual design can become 3d modeling, CGI/programming, drawing, painting, animation, environment design.

Game design can be programming and math.

Sound design can be musical composition, math, and programming.

A human life is short relative to the time required to master just *one* of these many crafts. Beethoven played and composed until he died.

Mastery is elusive enough. Someone may commit their life to a craft and only become decent, but not exceptional.

Some game developers choose to focus only on the programming, and hire artists to help them. I wonder if the harsh division of roles hurts the cohesion of the ultimate experience.

Others choose to focus only on the art and hire programmers or use engines to help them. I can't help but think that the programmer or engine is doing most of the work, and that *how good the game can be* is significantly limited by that programmer or engine, not by the artist contracting the project. If the programmer suddenly leaves, they will be hard to replace.

I think one who has dabbled a lot in many crafts may be able to manage projects better. I also hear that some very good managers in the film industry are very hands-off with talent that they hire, giving them room to work.

o

I'm a work-in-progress. So far, I've chosen to allocate my energetic youth to becoming decent in various crafts with lots of work. I think if I specialize later, having a diverse knowledge will help me *create* projects, rather than be a cog-in-a-wheel of a larger machine. Later, I will see how well this helps or hurts me. Perhaps pursuing combining crafts to create great big projects such as games is a worthy craft itself. Perhaps I'll think I should've specialized sooner. Perhaps not.

o

Eric Barone, developer of Stardew Valley, created the music, artwork, and gameplay code of his game.

Eric Barone versus Jonathan Blow on Game Engines.

A response by Eric Barone (creator of Stardew Valley) in a forum thread reads,

> "Is the a particular engine you are using or do you code from the ground up?"

> I've been coding Stardew Valley mostly from the ground up, using my own custom engine. There are certain features of the game that I've started to use 3rd party code for, however... for example, the low-level network functions for multiplayer. Also, XNA is kind of like a mini-engine, as it does take care of a lot of low-level stuff that would be a pain to do yourself (like taking an image you drew, importing it and turning it into an object you can work with in your code)... although it is all extremely general and could form the groundwork for any kind of game you'd imagine.

> "Is there any advice you could give a senior software developer who wants to dabble in game development?"

> Unless your game cannot be made otherwise, definitely use something like GameMaker. I know there might be an urge to prove oneself as a "real programmer" by making everything from scratch, but in the end it's not really worth it and it will drain

months of your life for no good reason. Of course, some projects are just too grand or unconventional and could not be made using GameMaker. I'm still not quite sure if I could've made Stardew using something like that, but it's too late now anyway... and true, now that I spent all the effort to do it myself the extra control and flexibility is nice. But if you are just starting out in game development you should probably be making small, simple games anyway.

(https://community.playstarbound.com/threads/game-development-and-engine-decision.25210/)

Eric Barone mentions an interesting point. "Unless your game cannot be made otherwise, definitely use something like *GameMaker*... Of course, some projects are just too grand or unconventional and could not be made using *GameMaker*."

I think it would be interesting to compare Eric Barone's thoughts to those of Jonathan Blow. It seems to me that Jon is pushing for mastery in his craft, while Eric Barone (and millions of fans) are satisfied with something that could already be made within the bounds of existing engines.

I've simplified a quote of Jonathan talking at the Worcester Polytechnic Institute, responding to the question "So why didn't you use Unity or Unreal?"

There's several reasons. Back when we started the game it wasn't even a consideration because they were so expensive. If you wanted to start using unreal back then, it was like $100,000 initially and 25% of everything you make. But even not considering that there's four reasons.

One is because we want to and it's very interesting.

Two is because when you're building something, want to be very precise about what you make. If I'm trying to make something that's delicate, it has to work. The way it's delicate is not necessarily technical, but really the way things feel... it's a long series of subtle things. I didn't know what they were ahead of time;

Five years later, finishing up the game, this particular thing isn't working, we need to change the way the engine works to do something else, and we were able to do that. If you license Unreal or Unity, (first you even have to have a source license, which most people don't have) then you're trying to modify something that is a great deal complex than if you only did what you game needs, because solving all problems for everyone [as game engines do] is a lot more complicated.

Three is I'm trying to make things that people

will be able to play in the future. You know, 20 years from now, which is not that long on the timetable of artistic works that we go back and appreciate.

I want people to be able to play the game, and how is that gonna work if it's on some version of Unity that's then one of 500 different incompatible version. Maybe somebody ported one of them, but it's not the particular one that the game is on, so then you have to port the game, but then it's broken because it doesn't totally feel the same, because something in the input system is different.

Four is not obvious especially when you're in school, but it becomes more obvious as you become a professional who's done some things and knows how it goes.

Unless you're doing something exactly that Unreal and Unity were built for, like "okay I want to make a first-person shooter in a few rooms and I'm not really stretching that capabilities of the engine at all." Then what those things do is they solve the easy problems, but they don't solve the hard problems, and the hard problems are what you really need help with in development.

Solving easy problems is nice, like "oh cool I ran this thing and just in the first day I got a guy on the screen and walking around!" That feels good, and that happens so that's why people use engines like that.

But getting a guy walking around on a screen is not the hard problem.

The hard problem is that when you're moving around a great deal, the load on the asset streaming system is huge; maybe asynchronously you have many probably hundreds of megabytes of textures and models and sound that has to be in memory at the right time based on transitions that happen.

That is not even what I would classify as a hard problem it just takes a lot of elbow grease and control over what's happening, and if you don't have enough control, you may not be able to do it with as tight of demands as we have.

It's not that important of a subject because I don't want to discourage beginners from using game engines, because if you're getting into games it'll help you it'll help you get started.

But I think if you're a serious practitioner, it's different. It's like I'm gonna paint a great painting and the canvas is made out of apple skin and it's probably gonna rot, and it's gonna take a great deal of work to restore this thing every 10 years...

You know, it's just not a good idea.

— Jonathan Blow (https://youtu.be/tRHnHIV96Jg?t=982)

I find the overlap and contrast of these two quotes fascinating.

Note what Jonathan says about why people use engines: "Solving easy problems is nice, like 'oh cool I ran this thing and just in the first day I got a guy on the screen and walking around!' That feels good, and that happens so that's why people use engines like that. But getting a guy walking around on a screen is not the hard problem." Eric Barone says he used a tool that does just that. It makes it easy to get a guy on the screen, walking around: "Also, XNA is kind of like a mini-engine, as it does take care of a lot of low-level stuff that would be a pain to do yourself (like taking an image you drew, importing it and turning it into an object you can work with in your code)." Already I see a square-peg round-hole effect with XNA doing asset management for you, that would make it more difficult to solve what Jonathan calls the hard problems: "The hard problem is that when you're moving around a great deal, the load on the asset streaming system is huge... if you don't have enough control, you may not be able to do it with as tight of demands as we have." I wonder if Eric's games just don't push the hardware enough to lend him a similar viewpoint to Jon.

Jon wanted to make a game on a big island. I remember hearing him mention that a lot of work had to go into making sure the whole island could render at once at a good frame-rate. Not only was this in 2014, but the consoles it released on had much stricter requirements than computers. This is relevant today because as hardware has gotten faster, the only thing that has changed is that we can make a bigger island, and we want to show more of it at once at a higher resolution. Rendering this island required a high level of control.

In terms of the level of control needed, I believe Eric Barone has little performance constraints but may have trouble getting the gameplay he wants. He expresses a consistent creative voice in Stardew Valley (2016) and Haunted Chocolatier (unreleased). Rendering both game's tile-maps is trivial even if done 1,000 times as inefficiently. Eric Barone mentions "I'm still not quite sure if I could've made Stardew using something like [GameMaker]." I think this may be related to the level of precision that Jon talks about. Many things like the movement feel[9] or scene management[10] might be clunkier in an engine; I believe these would change based on the engine used. He may have been inclined to use GameMaker's scene editor instead of whatever world editor he actually used, and perhaps that would have limited him differently and made a slightly different feeling game.

Both Jonathan and Eric agree that for *beginners*, engines may be good. Eric says after recommending GameMaker, "But if you are just starting out in game development you should probably be making small, simple games anyway." Jonathan says, "I don't want to discourage beginners from using game engines, because if you're getting into games it'll help you it'll help you get started." This is actually why I recommended Raylib at the start of this book. It makes it very easy to "get a guy on screen."

Someone may incorrectly think that an engine provides better utilities than Raylib or XNA or MonoGame for

---

9   Movement is always so integral to game feel, and yet I observe many people new to engines constrain themselves to what the engine's physics system can produce!

10 I personally have always found the scene management of engines to be very constrained; making transitions is usually a square-peg, round-hole situation that is much easier to manage without an engine.

physics or networking. This is false; you can use a headless physics library paired with your own engine or framework. Eric Barone touches this on networking, "There are certain features of the game that I've started to use 3rd party code for, however... for example, the low-level network functions for multiplayer." But regarding the cost of physics libraries: I believe this is a big deal, integral to game feel, and there's always an interfacing cost that *may* make it as bad as using an engine, so I wouldn't use a physics engine without serious deliberation of my goals.

To me, it seems if one can, it is a safe bet in the long-term to not use an engine. To make the best product, it makes sense that high precision in game-feel is required. Without an engine, a game may hold more longevity as work of art. Jon knows he could not have done what he did without an engine, and Eric Barone holds doubts that he could. However, both Jon and Eric don't find it a bad idea for beginners to use tools that can "get a guy on screen" quickly as it helps them get started.

Personally, I think that beginners, with as malleable brains as they have, would benefit from starting with powerful yet approachable tools like Raylib that can easily be upgraded later. If one starts with Godot or Unity, it will be harder to change to no engine, as Godot and Unity have very specific ways of doing things that would have no place in an engine-less game, and this may yet become a part of the way the developer thinks, having grown up on engines.

Try both.

For hundreds of hours.

If you don't pick one, you will starve.

Sometimes, there is a difficult choice. Should I use an engine, or should I not? Maybe you still haven't made up your mind. How could you know unless you had experience with both?

If you can afford to, it is good to try both. Make real projects with both.

But don't just spend ten hours with one, and a hundred hours with the other. The one with a hundred hours is slightly more likely to win, then. You should know the long-term nuances of both. With something such as game engines versus no engine, it is hard to waste your time, because if a hundred hours on engines would have hurt you, a hundred hours without engines will undo it. Well, as long as you approach *both* as a fresh beginner and don't try to act clever with your previous experience. If you do lean too heavily on past assumptions, you may use an engine for 1000 hours, then "not using an engine" might just end up with you wasting time re-making the game engine with a generic entity system, instead of simply drawing a player.

Boxes intersecting.

Collision can become complex but here's a basic picture that can get you going.

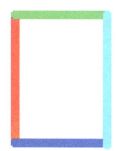

Notice the picture of the box to the right.

How do we know if a point is inside this box?

Well, if the point is right of the red wall, and left of the aqua wall, and below the green wall, and above the blue wall, then it is inside of the box. Try visualizing this with the picture.

What about two boxes? How do we know if they are intersecting?

Study the picture to the right.

Well, if
    the lime   wall is right of the red   wall,
and the orange wall is right of the blue   wall,
and the purple wall is above the yellow wall,
and the pink   wall is above the green wall,
then, they are intersecting.

This did not come intuitively to me at first as a kid, but

over time and many projects, it became easy to imagine.

I didn't *need* it to come intuitively, really. I just copied this function from project-to-project, with variations:

```
bool intersecting(float aMinX,  float aMinY,
                  float aWidth, float aHeight,
                  float bMinX,  float bMinY,
                  float bWidth, float bHeight)
{
    float aMaxX = aMinX + aWidth;
    float aMaxY = aMinY + aHeight;
    float bMaxX = bMinX + bWidth;
    float bMaxY = bMinY + bHeight;
    return (aMaxX >= bMinX && aMaxY >= bMinY &&
            bMaxX >= aMinX && bMaxY >= aMinY);
}
```

o

If you have a point moving towards a wall, you may not want to put it inside the wall. What if you want it to collide?

In the image on the right, imagine the point's Y is "p.y"

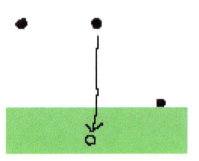

Imagine the ground's Y is "ground.y"

Imagine the ground's Y is less than the point's Y.

If after a move, p.y < ground.y, then set p.y = ground.y. If you want to use how deep it went into the wall so add some opposite-direction-bounce-velocity, you can calculate that before resetting the move with distance_inside = (ground.y – p.y)

(The previous calculation was done assuming that the ground is infinitely wide and tall. For a finite wall, you'll need constraints for both axes, not just the Y axis, and in both directions, not just for whether you're above it.)

There's a more complex version of this math that can support points hitting arbitrarily rotated rectangles, using vectors and dot-products.

I'm not a math teacher. I only know enough to help myself. While Casey Muratori is also not a math teacher, I believe he is good at explaining this. I recommend you check out Days 42-44 of Handmade Hero[11] for some information on that.

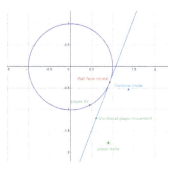

https://www.desmos.com/calculator/glwbvh1hix

---

11   https://guide.handmadehero.org/code/day042/

Discovering *Lerp*.

I was 12 years old. I signed off for the day, excited to work on my own top-down RPG from scratch in Java. I wanted to replicate the smooth movement of characters that RPG-maker games had, but could not think of an elegant way to do so.

I knew I could have separate variables; one for the player's tile position, and one screen-drawn position which tries to catch up to where the tile position should be drawn. Add 1 to the X or Y every frame, and soon we'll reach the destination with a simple `screen_position.x > target_screen_position.x` and be able to stop! But if I want to do that faster (perhaps 10 pixels per frame), then it might be imprecise, and if I clamp the value to never cross the target position, then it will suddenly move less pixels for one frame, which will make the speed seem weird. I want to make a good-feeling game, though!

So that night, the problem in my head. Assuming we have separate screen-space and tile-space coordinates, if the player's X position is 10 and their target X is 20, how can we smoothly move between then and the target in one second? If we know that we are 0.2 seconds into the animation, can we know where we need to be?

Okay, well, I know that 50% of the way between 10 and 20 is 15. That's half-way. Sounds good.

50% times 10 is 5. Then if I add the minimum value, it should work correctly because: 100% times 10. Then add the minimum value (10). 10 + 10 = 20. That means 100% is 20. Okay, and is the same true for 0%? 0% times 10 is 0. Then add the minimum value. 0 + 10 = 10. This is getting exciting!

So if I am 0 seconds into this animation, my X will be 10. If I am 1 second into this animation, my X will be 20. Wow! This sounds like what I need!

After that line of thought, I then made it work for any range of numbers, not just between 10 and 20. I realized that just take a percentage of 10 and then add any number. Like 50 + (10*percentage) gives an output range of [50,60] for a percentage range of 0% to 100%.

Then I found I don't need to multiply by 10; if the number is between 10 and 30, then half-way is 20: 10 + 20*0.5 gives the half-way number. I realized this number multiplied by the percentage is the range. Max minus minimum. 30-10 = 20.

That night, as a 12-year-old child, I discovered this ubiquitous function without knowing its name.

```
function lerp(float minimum, float maximum, float
percentage) {
  float range = maximum - minimum;
  return minimum + (range * percentage);
}
```

My knowledge that I could make a timer allowed me to think that I could use the seconds-into-the-animation to find the position to draw the character at, instead of adding to the position each frame as I already knew how to do.

Your knowledge will build, and you will be able to think in more complex ways. It will be rad.

A year later, when I was trying to make scroll-bars work for my tile puzzle game, my math wasn't working. It was frustrating. Me being a kid, I had little emotional involvement in whether or not I would do what was needed to get the work

done. I simply did the best I could. So, I took a walk outside, thinking it would help me think about the problem. And I discovered that scroll-bars are just an inverse lerp! If the minimum X position is 200 pixels, and the maximum is 400 pixels, then 50% is 300 pixels. It's the opposite of a lerp! Being a kid who hadn't even done algebra yet, I did not re-arrange my lerp algebraically as you may. I instead worked it out logically with my own thought process.

The actual code I wrote in the project became

```
element.cur = Math.round((((mouseX-element.x) /
element.w) * (element.max - element.min)) *
element.rounding)/element.rounding + element.min;
```

Which is basically the following, ignoring the above's special cases (such as rounding to the nearest *n* and scroll-bar minimum and maximum values).

```
function get_lerp_progress(float minimum, float
maximum, float current) {
  float width = maximum - minimum;
  return (current - minimum) / width;
}
```

o

This "then 50% is" problem-solving statement was pure luck, but it really clicked in my brain for solving these problems. But if that didn't work, I would have continued trying many very different things until one worked. That's what I was doing to even come up with "then 50% is" in the first place. Cast a wide net.

Me discovering *lerp* (the linear interpolation function) is just one of many things I've discovered on my own. Resources are helpful, but discovering things on your own allows you to exist independent of the quality of input you consume, and I believe in an imperfect human-driven society, that is valuable. Plus, how will you ever do anything interesting if you are only able to do what has been done before?

Eric Barone on art.

Also, if you plan on doing your own graphics... practice like crazy, study other games closely and think hard about what makes you like/hate their graphics. After dabbling for a while so that you have a mental framework to start from, read some pixel art tutorials. (here is a good one, although a little brief: http://www.pixeljoint.com/forum/forum_posts.asp?TID=11299).

Another thing... analyze games closely to figure out what's fun and not fun about them... you want your game to be fun!

— Eric Barone, creator of *Stardew Valley*

I like that Eric uses the word *after* in relation to dabbling and using tutorials. He does not say start with tutorials. Following his advice, you would spend a lot of time doing your own thing, and only *then* would you see what others have said. He says this is because it gives you a mental framework to start from...

I've spent at least 400 hours intensely studying hundreds of paintings. I really pushed myself to understand their composition and color. I would try to re-invent the same colors of the original artwork through observation alone. In my reproductions, I would see what I could take away and still have the same impact of the original piece. I would compare the brightness of the gray-scale versions of the paintings, and compare that to the non-gray-scale versions.

This study was invaluable. However, the only thing I would change is doing more of my own work between each study, as then I would have soaked up the valuable information in front of me better, and I would be able to better tell what is valuable and what is not.

o

This motif of spending time not reliant on tutorials seems to be prevalent in many people who are successful. They are able to gain the knowledge that one cannot learn from books.

Solve the problems that make your program interesting.

This chapter title is a quote from Jonathan Blow.

Your game only needs to look as fancy as it needs to before you work out making it fun or cool or interesting. Don't waste a bunch of time on graphics if you know you can do that later.

You might make a generic entity system. But have you made the game fun yet? And if after 10 hours you finish your entity system you finally realize the idea you had isn't very fun, then that was a waste of time.

A simple, un-detailed painting can be strong. It's not very much risk to work a lot furthering a painting that has already proven it has something.

A painter usually blocks in big broad important ideas before working to details.

A writer may have key points in their head before they write a draft — the draft containing improper grammar and constantly-changing past/present tense. Verb tense can be fixed later. Fundamental ideas will require a whole re-write.

A game developer makes something fun or cool, and then they build on that.

There's ways to waste time. These are things that are inconsequential. Doing them made no difference.

There's ways to use time. These are things that were integral to the product, and that the product could not have been done in any other way for.

Sometimes I sit down for a programming session, and I wonder what I should work on. "Solve the problems that make your program interesting" makes it obvious and easy to draw from my past experience.

The Indie Game Jam (a manifesto of game design)

Home | SF.net Page | IGJ0 | IGJ1 | IGJ2

The Indie Game Jam is a yearly game design and programming event **designed to encourage experimentation and innovation in the game industry**. A very small volunteer team of professional game developers creates a new custom game engine with a single technology focus, and then we invite a slightly larger group of game programmer-designers to get together and make as many innovative games as possible over a four-day period. The games are shown at the Experimental Gameplay Workshop at the Game Developers Conference, and the code is released on SourceForge under the GNU General Public License, so everyone can freely experiment with the engine source code and games.

Sponsored by:

 Indie Game Jam 2 took place March 18 through March 21st, 2004, in Oakland, California. **21 game developers** made **17 experimental and innovative games** over the course of 4 days!

 Indie Game Jam 1 took place the following year, from February 28th through March 3rd, 2003 and surpassed all expectations for the second year in a row! **17 game developers** created **18 experimental and innovative games** in 4 days!

 Indie Game Jam 0 took place March 15th through 18th, 2002, in Oakland, California, and it was an amazing success! **14 game developers** created **12 experimental and innovative games** in 4 days!

Machines generously loaned by Intel

Hosting and source code control provided by

Also see the Lithuanian Game Developers Jam-Session

Chris Hecker <checker'at'd6.com>, Thatcher Ulrich <igj'at'tulrich.com>, Justin Hall <justin'at'bud.com>,

(http://www.indiegamejam.com/)

If the goal is to make interesting game that last hundreds of years, it can be boring to code a camera and an inventory and an entity system and write the same shaders within a window that updates 60 times a second.

The original Indie Game Jam started in 2002 was to make things interesting and innovative.

> This year we're going to be doing games using Zack Simpson et al.'s "Shadow Garden" system. It's a wacky and cool interaction and presentation platform, it's significantly different from last year...

> Shadow Garden, in its fully setup form, is comprised of a projector (like an LCD projector for PowerPoint presentations), a screen/surface to project onto, a camera, and the software. The camera is off to the side or above, and aimed at the screen. The player stands between the projector and the screen, casting a shadow onto the screen. The camera sees the player's shadow on the screen, and the software reacts to the person's shadow in interesting ways by drawing stuff either into a bitmap or with OpenGL.

> The SG system has plugins for individual games/experiences. So, for example, there are plugins that have sand drop from the top of the screen and pile up on the player's shadow. Little creatures can hide under the shadow, and if you move fast enough you reveal them. Butterflies land

on the shadow if you hold still. You get the idea. You can see examples and videos of some of the plugins at http://www.mine-control.com.

— Chris Hecker

Bird flying game. Your arms are wings.

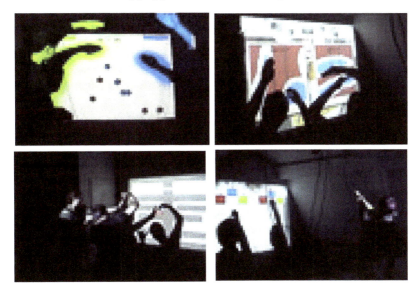

I haven't seen what these other games do; what's important to me is that they're pursuing an entirely different way of making games in many ways. This is why standard game engines are sometimes boring.

I'm not cut out for this.

You might just be looking for ways to not succeed while telling yourself you tried your hardest.

— Jonathan Blow, creator of *Braid* and *The Witness*

An excuse; excuses are things we say to ourselves because we want to make sure we do not succeed.

Some people start with early brain connections that make certain things easy (the idea of "talent"). Some people start at a young age, so they develop those connections quickly (kids on pianos).

Maybe if you stayed who you are now, you will not succeed. Maybe. If you think that is true, then all you need to do is change your behaviours. It need not happen overnight, but perhaps it need happen.

If I stayed who I was as a kid, I would not be accomplishing very much. I did the motions of people who create; I drew comics, I put colors together to make paintings, I programmed, I posed stick figures in animations—

But I never did it well, nor did I care very much about doing it well. I simply did it for fun, and then quit when I wanted to play a game instead.

I wasn't cut out for succeeding at anything I tried. Yet.

Because we can grow and change and pick up bad habits and throw the bad habits off again.

Someone who thinks they aren't cut out for this has simply given up. Excuses are toxic: they feed themselves. If you think that, then it is true. If you do not, then it is not. If something's not working, then just change it.

O

The people around me influenced me. When I started surrounding myself with people who really care about their craft (such as Hayao Miyazaki), it allowed me to grow.

When I find someone who has a cool energy, I like to look for interviews, documentaries, or podcasts they produce so I may enjoy their presence and steal their attitudes.

O

I don't think innate talent is a useful idea, if we're able and willing to change our brains in whatever way is necessary. Perhaps the only real talent is the ability to work hard. Not everyone can put their work beyond their emotions and get it done. Perhaps if one thinks they lack talent and therefore will not try, the real lack of talent is the lack of working hard.

You might have to become crazy.

Rick Rubin wrote a book on his relationship to creativity. To some, its ideas may seem crazy. Being a vessel that the universe flows ideas through.

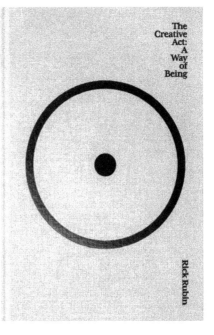

Religion allows us to be happy people who are kind and unafraid of death. It allows some people to become self-justified in horrible terrorism. It is versatile. Why not use religious-thinking for enhancing creativity?

Why not convince ourselves of certain ideas that are obviously false from our current world-view, but might lead to interesting results?

If I showed 10-year-old-me, whom I'm writing for, this book, then I know they'd think, "you're weird" 100 times.

Don't try to be crazy. But if being perceived as crazy is a side-effect to doing what you know is correct, then do not fear it. Crazy is just normal under a different lens.

This is what I mean when I say society is not set up to support mastery. Sometimes, the things I need to do are weird by the lens of people around me. But then it makes results, and only then people understand.

Working Hard & Romanticizing.

> Working hard should be a matter of course. Our line of work is filled with people who work hard but are no good as human beings. Placing value on the act of working hard is an incredible mistake.
>
> ...
>
> Working hard, it's just something you do. If you don't, nothing worthwhile will come about.
>
> Thinking about that, some people can't sleep at night. But that's a matter of course too. At times like that, I know that encouragement from other people, or comfort and consolation, aren't any help at all. It's all on you. In those moments, can you forgive yourself? Some people can forgive themselves easily, and some people can't.
>
> That's a difference that separates the fates of those two types of people. People who can easily forgive themselves don't do very good work.

— Hayao Miyazaki
(https://soranews24.com/2019/07/10/hayao-miyazaki-talks-on-how-working-hard-isnt-something-to-be-proud-of-not-forgiving-yourself/)

It's dark. A faint yellow light behind you illuminates a dark hall-way. Past that hallway, you hear the *tap-click-clack* of an old IBM keyboard. Turning a corner, you see a CRT monitor illuminating the face of a young Mark Zuckerberg. Cables strangle everywhere, and lights on the computer punch the darkness with red, green, and blue. He is creating *Facebook*.

If you thought that sounded cool, then that is good. If it did not, then I hope you have some other mental picture that romanticizes working hard and making things, whether it's games, wood-working, art, or something else.

This romantic fantasy I view like a carrot and stick. It does not really change what we have to do to make a game, but it changes my mental view. I feel I'm a part of something bigger. I feel I'm living in a fantasy, in real-life. This makes doing the same objective work easy.

There's another thing. It's the ability to push through strain. The ability to work hard. Ideally we do not have to do this much, but sometimes it is useful.

o

Regarding romantic fantasies, I've observed it may take very little for me to enjoy a lot of work. Just hearing one nice song for the first time can encourage me to change my world-view and look forward to something vague in the distant future. I see a great piece of work, and I wonder if I can produce something that connects to someone else such as that work did to me.

It reminds me of something *Man's Search for Meaning* explored: paradoxical intention. It may solve someone's 10 years of anxiety, or 10 years of grief, in one evening.

Sometimes we set up problems in our heads as if they are hard to solve. That itself may make it harder to solve and make a nasty feedback loop, but sometimes we're just using the wrong solutions.

This is so hard!

I came upon a rant by a relatively new programmer who is frustrated by the immensity of game development. They talk about how code is so boring compared to walking their dog and going to parties.

I think the ones who accomplish high success are crazy. Crazy enough that they would *rather* code than go to a party. Crazy enough that when confronted by an obstacle or excuse, they keep going. I think it's not so bad to be crazy, in this way.

Then again, I don't see why one can't just go to parties *and* code. I think this particular person really disliked programming.

Becoming a native speaker.

Adults who learn a language often sound like "foreigners." Children who learn a language sound like natives.

I put a lot of effort into trying to solve this disparity with myself. If I am to be multi-disciplined, I do not want to be like a foreigner in any discipline.

Foreigners often use sounds from their own language instead of using the second language's pronunciations. It's almost as if using what we know is harmful to being wholly immersed as a native.

Foreigners often think of something in their native language first, *then* try to translate it to the second language. This is a square-peg, round-hole.

I suppose I want to learn as a child does. Without pre-conceptions. Without pretensions. Willing to integrate new thought patterns into my being.

Some say they think in pictures and are visual learners. Others say they think in words. I seek to rise above all of that entirely; when I need to think in pictures, I will think in pictures (such as for painting). When I need to think in words, I will think in words. I am capable of both; it's just a muscle that needs to be strengthened.

To me, learning a language only to then not sound like a native is an example of dead-weight assumptions. You didn't learn it as if you were a child. Your existing knowledge and ability hurt your ability to speak this language natively. I think of this with every craft I approach.

How might you rectify the disparity that you will be a "foreigner" in the craft of game design or programming?

Deep knowledge and forgetfulness.

For me, deep knowledge is not something I need to remember. It's something that manifests in my brain because of its necessity. Understanding the time complexity of algorithms is an intuitive thing in my head, thanks to years of experience. If I forget it, my next project will make me remember it.

I suppose with experience and knowledge, you are able to craft new good ideas. So if you forget something and aren't able to craft it again, perhaps it wasn't a very good idea.

It's easy to start from a blank slate. If I were weighed down by all of what I've done, it would be hard to move forward.

o

I don't try to memorize all of the algorithms and data structures. I know how memory works. I know how to write algorithms. I rarely think "Oh! A perfect candidate for this is the linked list!" Rather, I think "it would be useful to chain these pointers for a very particular reason" and re-invent the linked-list from scratch. I don't want square-pegs and round-holes. If I am only limited to a small set of data structures, then I am limited to a bunch of variously shaped holes. That's non-ideal.

o

I don't need to know every nuance of how a thing works if it's such a good idea that, with my experience, I come up with it every time with no gripes.

Some people reference the name of the function they're typing. Other people simply type what they think the function should be called, and then change the name of the function if it isn't what they thought it should be.

Maybe it's time to rename "drawRectangle" to be what I thought it should be.

Some people are concerned with being correct and consistent. Others are concerned with being the best, even if they must defy the norm.

Throughout this book, I've mentioned "dead-weight assumptions" as something counter to good work. It is in forgetfulness that we find our opportunity to be rid of them.

o

One way I like to practice forgetfulness is by forgetting everything except that I want to accomplish a particular goal. The path I take can be anything, regardless of past experience.

Creating things the way they "should" be.

> "The less exposed you are to the way everybody else thinks, the more unique you'll be"

— James Gurney (https://youtu.be/5xkn7VWdKZ8?&t=5920)

I often struggled with the idea that I should have to make things a certain way. In my painting, should I put shadows under the grass? It would be realistic!

One great realization I had is that if it ruins the painting at an abstract level, then there is no point in the painting existing. Adding a "realistic" thing *can* destroy the painting. For me personally, the painting doesn't exist to be realistic. It exists to be pleasing. This is why I started painting.

People tell me to do certain things in various crafts. Sometimes it's objectively good advice. Other times, it's advice that can be misapplied. And knowing me, if advice *can* be misapplied, then I *will* misapply it.

I would make a Shakespearian tragedy by making this fake idea of dramatic irony in my head. I would go through with something that deep down I know is a bad idea, but I would rather do as I was told than do what was deep down the best thing. Sometimes I'm not thinking about the best possible thing for the project. Instead, I'm thinking about how to please only the people who know me, the creator, by doing what they want. That's my mistake, and it's a pattern. Avoid this, if you can. Do what will get you to where you want to be, and what will make the end result you want to make.

Lerp can make things tend towards a point.

My older brother, who dabbles lightly in game development, made a simple top-down 2D *Unity* prototype with a few collidable boxes and a dash ability. It was to be a stealth game.

He showed me what he had, and I saw that the camera almost looked like it had a camera man who followed the player. He showed me what he did, and it looked like this:

```
camera_position = lerp(camera_position,
player_position, 0.1);
```

I thanked him for showing me and went to do my research. It turns out "lerp" was a concept I already discovered! And he wasn't just doing it on a number, but on multiple at once (X and Y of a camera).

```
Vector2 lerp(Vector2 from, Vector2 to, float progress) {
    float resultX = from.x + (progress*(to.x - from.x));
    float resultY = from.y + (progress*(to.y - from.y));
    return (Vector2){ resultX, resultY };
}
```

I still use lerp to this day for making smooth continuous motions straight to moving target points that slow down as they reach their target point. It's very handy.

Easing functions

Lerps are cool. Imagine if you lerp from A to B by different percentages per frame:

Frame 1	0%	O			
Frame 2	10%		O		
Frame 3	50%			O	
Frame 4	90%				O
Frame 5	100%				O

Over time, that makes a cool speed-up and slow-down effect! How about this:

Frame 1	0%	O			
Frame 2	5%	O			
Frame 3	15%		O		
Frame 4	50%			O	
Frame 5	100%				O

It looks like it's speeding up!
(https://easings.net/) is a good reference for this. It tells you what math can transform a linear progress from 0-1 into the special curve. Such as `progress = x*x` giving you a "speeding up" effect (easeInQuad)

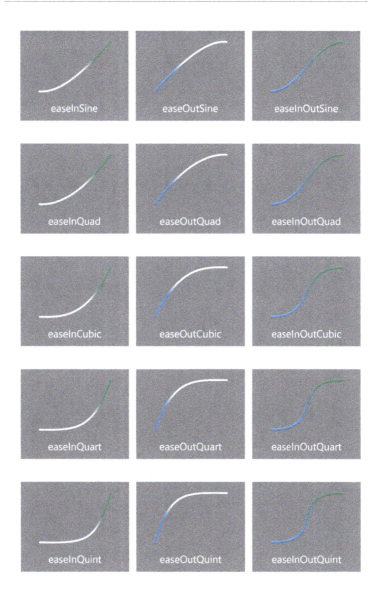

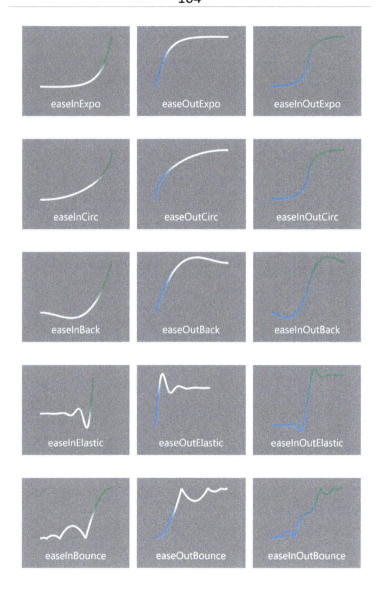

Code is malleable.

Are you scared of writing bugs? No worry. Just fix them.

Are you scared that your game won't be able to do as much as you want? No worry. Just change your game.

Are you scared that your code may not support what you want in future? No worry. Just make it simple now, so you can change it later trivially.

Don't try to plan for every future case. Don't write complicated stuff where it does not need to be complicated.

I'm willing to re-write a project 10 times if it's not good. I'm willing to re-write specific parts of the project if there are new features I want to support. I try to make it easy to change things in my code-base. I try to make things simple and understandable while still supporting the complexity they do.

Here's how I handle scenes in my game.

```
if state.scene == GameScene.Level
{
    update_and_render_level(state);
}
else if state.scene == GameScene.JourneyMap
{
    update_and_render_journey_map(state);
}
else if state.scene == GameScene.LevelEditor
{
    update_and_render_level_editor(state);
}
else if state.scene == GameScene.VoxelEditor
{
    update_and_render_voxel_editor(state);
}
```

It's pretty simple. I have an if statement. Based on if a number is 0 (Level), 1 (JourneyMap), 2 (LevelEditor), or 3 (VoxelEditor), I do different code.

Some people want you to do complicated things with "polymorphism" that involves making each scene a class and giving it a generic interface to use.

This project is currently 35,000 lines long. I can't afford that kind of complexity that would slow me down. I need everything that can be simple to be simple.

Marathon.

Games can be huge. I've been working on *Journey to Royn* for a year and a few months. I am a different person to who I was before. This is a long time for a young person because they undergo many changes in their understanding, brain-development, and hormones.

When I finished the puzzle game *Winterfrost* in a week for a game jam and worked many hours — 10 efficient hours a day — I wasn't able to make it as good as I was able to. I really tried. But with the hours I put into the parallax falling snow, lighting, and parallax squares in the background, I had little time for level design and making the core mechanics more interesting. The shop items were bland. There simply wasn't enough time to do it all.

So, games take a long time to make. A simple 2D game could not be good in 70 hours[12].

---

12 I discount the idea that the frameworks I used slowed me down as I believe it would have taken similar time without frameworks, drawing from my current experience mostly not using them. I also discount the idea that fatigue from working long hours slowed my efficiency down; I was young and energetic and excited. I am surprised remembering just how directly I attacked problems with vigour.

Knowing how to make games is as important as being able to do it. If you are motivated now, then now is a great time to set yourself up mentally to keep at this for a long time.

o

Jonathan Blow recounts that when he worked on Braid, he took Tai Chi classes. I believe he said that without them, he would not have been able to complete the game in exactly the way he did (perhaps there would be other life-style changes required to work as much as he did).

o

Regarding generally managing yourself: I know little of the human body, but society has me believe it is important to be exposed to direct sun-light, exercise, and eat balanced meals. By my experimentation, these have worked well for me. I do not drink coffee as it seems a drug; people addicted to it have to drink it just to be normal, due to the body becoming reliant on this external source of energy and no longer manufacturing its own. Perhaps it could be useful in moderation.

I do things outside of work every day that support me mentally. I re-watch documentaries that I enjoyed, such as *10 Years with Hayao Miyazaki.* I watch streams of other programmers programming. Seeing people chase their crafts makes what I do feel meaningful, while I am not surrounded by anyone who would find the craft deeply meaningful. I do radio calisthenics to help my body's circulation and make me happier.

o

Sometimes the old things don't work any more. The ability to adapt to new things is as important as the ability to do things. My attachment to ways of spending time is counter to completing the marathon.

Perhaps a good thing is to wait until you objectively observe a negative pattern with yourself, then you know it is time to make a change. Life can be exciting.

You can't both own a cake and eat it.

Once I heard Jonathan Blow discussing how some people don't like Linus Torvalds and himself because they can be grumpy about shoddy work. I remember a possible conclusion which is that if you take away that person's grumpyness, then maybe you took away what made them good in the first place.

Hayao Miyazki says some people can easily forgive themselves, and so they don't do very good work. Maybe forgiving yourself and others for doing bad work can help you sleep at night, but it will not help your end results. Of course, in the same quote, Miyazaki started by saying "Our line of work is filled with people who work hard but are no good as human beings. Placing value on the act of working hard is an incredible mistake;" he attempts to emphasize how we value ourselves as human beings as coming first. It seems he believes that being a good human being and being a producer of good work aren't necessarily connected (being orthogonal).

I don't mind being passionate about work and refusing to feel good about bad work (where it wasn't even useful to fail). I don't value people based on the quality of work they do. It's just separately kind of cool to do quality work.

Wow, quittin' time already?

If I am very motivated, work will come easily. When I decide to quit will form a habit. I spent 9 hours straight writing this book today. It came very easily because I am very motivated right now. This motivation is rare; it is the motivation of a new project — of a new future. If I made myself stop at the 3rd hour, and then the next day made myself stop at the 3rd hour, and I continued that for two weeks, 9 hours of work straight would seem unthinkable. Quitting is a habit.

Right now, I schedule myself to work for two 3-hour blocks every day of the week. By the end of the 3rd hour, my brain is already ready to quit.

I have a theory that the way we use the time is a habit as well. That is one reason I started this 3-hour-time-blocks schedule; I wanted to practice powerful bursts of energy followed by rest.

I wonder whether working hard is just a matter of habit. I saw a person who who drew for hours every day on schedule, producing often. When they had a Repetitive-Strain-Injury that prevented them from drawing, it was devastating. They were prevented from working hard not by their brain but by their body. I wonder if what they felt is like what an addicted gamer feels when the internet or power turn off. I certainly have held myself to work schedules and felt strong negativity on days where I was late to it, not because I felt like I had to feel like that to be stronger, but because it was just what I did. In this, I remember a portion of the Miyazaki quote from the chapter "Working Hard & Romanticizing"

> Working hard, it's just something you do.

Maybe it's just a life-long habit for some people. I really do not know.

It's for an audience.

Even if the audience is yourself.

When I was 9 years old, I remember toying with *Cinema 4D* for animation. My animations were awful. They would be over in about 3 seconds, the camera would travel ten meters in that time, and the characters would go from a state of conflict to riding off to the sunset. In three seconds.

You could say the issue is that I didn't have a sense of timing. But really, if I had been thinking of how the film would be perceived as an end-product, "having a sense of timing" would become natural and automatic. I see that as the real issue.

The experience of creating may be different than the experience of consuming, but consideration should be given to how the creation experience will influence the an

"He's walking forward so his leg should move up, right?" 12 frames overlaid of a 0.5 second animated scene made when I was 9 years old.

audience member's consumption experience.

It works. Why change it?

Some creatives strive for something far beyond what has already been done. What will survive in history — the candy someone enjoyed making, or the dawn of the newest, freshest, most unique candy? Creativity can be pushing the boundaries of what we know. It can also be producing cotton candy.

For most people, good enough is good enough. Often when I observe successful creatives, they pushed for more, especially when it was not the safest choice to do so.

Hayao Miyazaki produced a wildly successful film titled "*My Neighbor Totoro*." Its bright theme and its target audience of children brought it to success. Later, he surprised himself by writing a dark film for adults about a man who designed planes that kill people. His wife asked, "Why don't you make something like *Totoro*?" Miyazaki retorted, "But I already made *Totoro*."

In this case, I believe the goal is beyond financial success. In contrast, one could look at Thomas Kinkade, whose paintings of cottages by a river earned him hundreds of millions of dollars. Many art critics call his paintings bland.

Regarding the chapter title, one's goal may be creative success in pushing boundaries. In that case, it may not work, and must be changed.

Contemporary art.

Games are art.

We only remember the best things from the past. Everything else is largely forgotten, except for the brains of the few art historians. However, everything that is contemporary is very exciting and popular. Everyone loves the new thing.

Once the new thing becomes the old thing, it takes its place in art history and is rated fairly among other old works.

Games are strange. Right now, many people have lived as long as the art form. If games started in the 1950s, then it has been 70 years from this book's time. I think we may lack this context that we are contributing to what will be a craft practised for thousands of years.

Contemporary stuff seems cool now, but I wish I could see what is "contemporary" (now) in 1,000 years.

I want to make an engine that helps me make games!

I've made many an engine and framework for myself. In reflection, I see that I would finish the framework project, make a simple game with it, and then realize its limitations and start my next project without the framework.

If you want to make a game (and you're not trying to support any team members who do not know how to program), just make it without making your own framework abstraction layer.

If you want to not re-write the same code from project-to-project as much, then start using the copy-paste feature. An example of a successful person doing this is Jonathan Blow, who I believe copied code from *Braid*'s level editor into *The Witness*'s editor, and then copied code from *The Witness*'s level editor and animation file format parser into his currently unreleased sokoban game.

For me, it can be fun to pursue excitement, and disappointing to not. It would just be helpful if the excitement is placed in things that help serve the craft.

Game jams and burnout.

Game jams were cool. I had good experiences with them. Great excuse to iterate on ideas quickly. It's a way to meet people. I also found I could burn out a lot. For one particular game jam —the hardest I've worked — I worked for 10 hours a day for a week. I was happy. After the game jam ended, I wanted to work more. I really wanted to make cool things.

But everything that I wanted to do seemed like so much effort. It was like I could sit down to do the thing, and then every line of code felt monumental. Every bit of conceptual art ate a large amount of energy. I really wanted to work.

It's like when you go to sleep, and you wake up, and you're still mentally exhausted.

For me, this lasted for 3 months, starting in December 2021. Though it could have been mitigated.

I worked lightly during that 3 month burnout. Just fun things. I designed for animations and practiced my hand-drawn animation.

o

During early February, I played a video game *World of Tanks* for 10 hours a day for a week for a "WZ-114 marathon." Video games almost let us not solve our life's problems. I don't know what anti-depressants are like, but if I had to guess, I would imagine they are like playing an addictive video game for longer than is fun. I've used it for deliberately forgetting about things that make me angry or anxious that would feed me to think about those things again which make me more angry or anxious.

o

This burnout was a catalyst for me to begin studying the craft of picture-making in more detail than I had before. I remember hearing of a study of dopamine in rats. Rats with the dopamine center of the brain removed would have food placed in front of them, then starve to death without the motivation to get the food.

However, *importantly,* when researchers placed sugary food in the mouth of the same rat who would rather starve, the rat exhibited pleasure chemicals in its brain. Dopamine was only the motivator to *get* pleasure, but if the rat did something pleasurable, it would still feel pleasure.

In deep depression or confusion, it can help one to force themselves to do something they think is objectively good or could lead to a fun thing in hindsight, even though they do not want to do it.

Learned Helplessness

When I learned what learned helplessness was, I immediately recognized it in myself and hated it and changed very quickly.

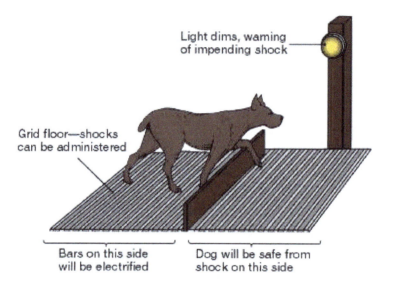

Light dims, warning of impending shock

Grid floor—shocks can be administered

Bars on this side will be electrified

Dog will be safe from shock on this side

A basic experiment to describe the idea is that a dog is on a floor that can be electrified to cause discomfort for the dog. The dog learns that only one of the two rooms it can be in will be shocked. So, it crosses to the other room in order to avoid the shock.

Then, after the dog has learned to hop to the other room when a shock starts in their current room, the researchers shock both rooms at once. The dog finds that if they cross to the other room, they are still being shocked. Eventually they lie down in discomfort. They learned there is nothing they can do.

Here's the worst part. The researchers then go back to the initial procedure of the experiment: only one room is shocked at once. However, given up, the dog does not attempt to cross to the other room; the dog has learned to be helpless.

I think it is useful for me to hate the idea of this in myself. I *should* think about learned helplessness and think "I should change my behaviours and avoid that!"

Will-power as a muscle.

I've heard some liken will-power to a muscle.

I've observed that when I make a habit of doing something productive for 30 minutes a day, after enough days I want to do it for 60 minutes a day, because 30 minutes feels too little. Then, after that, I want to do it for 120 minutes a day because I don't have enough time to do all I want to do. I would eventually have a habit of working for 6 hours a day, and then during the unscheduled time, I would work even more if I could, without taking weekends as breaks as most do. This certainly has worked decently for me.

I can't help but wonder about better ways. I feel I top-out too soon, and that I can't consistently work for as high as 12 hours a day. Successful people I observe are able to *live* working hard. This is my personal disparity that I am looking to resolve. Perhaps you could compare your own situation to mine and learn something.

o

I mentioned no weekends as breaks. If one's pretension to living is only to stop, I wonder what they're giving up. Could they enjoy living through their work? This may not be for everyone, but it's certainly over-done in our culture that we work for 5 days a week and take 2 days off.

Sharp tools.

People are scared of C and assembly. "What if I write the wrong code? Or worse! What if I dereference a null pointer!" Here's the deal. I dereference null pointers all the time. Most of the time it's intentional. When it's not, my debugger tells me that I did anyway, and then I track down the bug and fix it.

```
#define assert(condition) { if(!(condition))
{ *((u8*)0) = 0; } }
```

When you have a sharp tool, you may cut yourself. When you cut yourself, you learn.

There are things you cannot fail at. Such as driving. If you fail at driving, you endanger your life as well as others.

In video games, programming, painting, animation, and music, I hope you set yourself up such that failing is *affordable*. It's very useful to learn from.

Isn't this pretty?

```c
#include <stdint.h>
typedef uint8_t u8;
typedef uint16_t u16;
typedef uint32_t u32;
typedef uint64_t u64;
typedef int8_t s8;
typedef int16_t s16;
typedef int32_t s32;
typedef int64_t s64;
```

If I want to make an unsigned 8-bit number, I can explicitly type:

```c
u8 number = 0;
```

Growing up with "int" and "short" and "long" and "long long" which are totally indescriptive makes this seem nice.

You can make your code-bases reflect ways you like doing things. In C, this can be with `typedef`s or `#define`s. Of course, this has little bearing on whether or not one will complete a good project. Rather, it's just the type of thing one sees on a human-interest news show, or on a tweet. A bit of fun for fun's sake.

Being a creator in an age of consumption.

I could be on *Twitter* (now known as 𝕏) all day. I could scroll on *TikTok* or watch *YouTube* videos a lot. It feels all society wants me to do is that.

Advertising. Never do I feel more like a consumer than with an advertisement. I feel all the companies want me to do is feel comfortable with giving them money. As if that should be my primary motivation in life. It truly feels like hypnosis. I would be more malleable to it if I weren't so disgusted by this idea.

One way to be a creator in an age of consumption is to consume things at least related to crafts of creation. This is watching *YouTube* videos by painters and animators.

Another way is to circumvent the consumption entirely. It's when I've felt a sense of community and belonging with fellow artists that I was able to completely give up video games and watching YouTube videos for months. For me, having grown up on video games, this was a big deal, and it has stuck with me since: I am no longer addicted to video games. They are not a source of pleasure.

One thing I've tried is protecting my time. In the past, I allocated two hours every morning to improving my craft of drawing. Another thing I tried is "no internet until 4 p.m." I found I re-watched physical media I had a lot during that time. If, during internet time, I downloaded something to watch during no-internet time, it was a deliberate choice that it would be meaningful. There was no "doom-scrolling" or endless *Reddit* browsing.

o

Being a creator involves being able to put in the work. I feel as I became an adult, I gained the mental ability to do things that aren't *like eating candy* more.

o

The social media algorithms choose what we consume. It's not a person who wants good for the world. It's not a magazine editor. It's incentivised to show incendiary comments with no context that obviously make people angry.

For me, this was good incentive to realize I should be careful with which algorithms I fall victim to.

o

Growing up in consumer culture, I can't help but want to be a consumer. Some are more fortunate; some are born into environments and communities where creating cool things and doing a good job are encouraged. If one is not born into this environment by luck, they may seek it out. For me, community motivates desire.

o

If you ever pondered getting off of social media for your own good, then now is the time. Tell your friends how they can contact you. Rid yourself of obligations to log in. Change your password to something hard to type and don't even write it down; you'll have to use a password reset if you ever log in again.

Some may benefit from not stopping immediately. Withdrawal of dopamine might be immense; one could limit their time every day lower and lower, until they _jump_ from 30 minutes a day to none. That jump is when they may say goodbye and change their password.

Now, it can be scary to have free time without an easy answer of how to spend it. It need not be replaced with hard things; after all, social media was just our brain trying to find an easy way to spend time; I simply find it good to not be beholden to the inflammatory dopamine treadmill that is social media. Definitely _don't_ replace social media with reading news about wars and deaths that you have no involvement with. It's doom-scrolling all over again.

Syntax Highlighting.

This is near the back of the book for a reason. It's not a valuable discussion and whether or not you use syntax highlighting has very little bearing on whether or not you will be successful. What will have an impact of your success is how much you care about it. There are things you can care about that will make a huge impact to the end product. And there are things that you can care about that might make a popular tweet, but will not do anything meaningful.

I liked seeing Sean Barrett's setup. Monochrome C code looked like candy. I was good at word-searches as a kid; perhaps that's a factor. From then on, I never used syntax highlighting for serious purposes again. Rob Pike, creator of the *Go* programming language, does not either. It took 1 month to get used to, after 8 years of rainbow code.

Sean Barrett explains his GPU compute shader voxel raycasting engine (https://youtu.be/DW93P4bZJIo)

Chancing success.

Imagine there is a 5% success-rate at something. If this is a 5% success-rate at the moon landing, then that is scary because astronauts might die a horrible death.

If there is a small chance of success for writing and pitching a novel, and it turning out to be good and appreciated by people because it's good, then that's awesome and let's do it hundreds of times until it succeeds once. It can be useful to fail sometimes, because you chanced success. But other times, there was no chance of success and something needs to change.

o

Financial success isn't really the goal: why would we be making games or doing any creative craft if we wanted money? That's a _horrible_ idea. If I wanted deep financial success, I would have picked a better career.

If financials were a goal, then are always choices that make an inferior product in favour making more money. If you don't care about the craft or good products, then you probably could have chosen a better way of making money.

My goal is to explore my chosen crafts, understand them well, and make things of meaning. The good thing is this can bring supporting financials if done well.

o

Jonathan Blow talks about how after working on his hover-tank game around the 2000s, he was $100,000 USD in debt. He and a business partner split the debt and worked to pay it off.

Then, to independently fund *Braid* and avoid publishers which induce creative pressure, he did freelance work for companies.

Then with the success from *Braid*, he funded *The Witness* for a few million dollars.

Then, after the success from *The Witness* and working on a programming language and game for 8 years, he said, "Nothing is more frustrating than instead of using $20,000,000 to go relax on an island, spending it on making this game only to hire someone who refuses to do the work he was paid to do."

Separately, he has said that he only cares about money enough to make better games, and hearing others worry about whether a game will succeed is a big waste of energy.[13] He cares about making good games, not successful games.

---

13 https://youtu.be/PCjG-xr3RkA

Your journey continues.

The end of this book need not end the impact of its ideas. Hopefully what you take away from this will help you for the better; if not, I encourage you to forget what does not help you; be rid of dead-weight assumptions.

I hope you enjoyed your experience reading this. I love reading books like this, and yet I've never seen a book share such particular ideas as this one has.

Send me an email at `michael.gpq@gmail.com` if you would like to say hello, share your thoughts, or have any questions! Perhaps, having read the whole book, this will be a fun way of closure for you.

Resources.

The best programming education out there right now.
https://handmadehero.org/

Communities for asking questions and seeing/showing progress. (I see none of these as ideal for mastery in game design and they may steer you off course, but they're probably fun. *Handmade Network* is especially good for general programming discussion and advice.)
https://handmade.network/
https://forums.tigsource.com/
https://gamedev.net/

Fun and motivational. From the creator of *Heartbound,* a website encouraging you to make games and lending some tips.
https://develop.games/

Regarding mastery, I recommend you seek out people who are at the top of their crafts and look for interviews, podcasts, and talks by them. If we become like those we surround ourselves with, this is not a bad course.

Perhaps it's even better to not be dependant on those around us, though this I have not figured out how to do to good effect yet.

Fun fact: the chapter titled **Just give me a draw rectangle function. I will make the game.** is a reference to Hayao Miyazaki worrying he will die of old age before completing a film, when a director friend of his quenched his worries by saying, "Finish the storyboards. I will finish the film."